CONFESSIONS
OF A
THIEF

TRUE EVENTS

TRUMAN BUCKLES

Contents

Prologue: The First Taste for Thievery

This book tells the true story of a family of seven brothers and seven sisters. All the sisters worked hard and went to school and, over time, made something out of themselves. Of the seven brothers, three were half-brothers. The reason I tell you this is because it plays a very important part in this book, which speaks of how money can cause love to turn to hate and destroy a family.

I guess just about everyone loves their mother, and I am proud to say our mother was special. She loved every one of us the same, and no matter how poor we were, she made sure there was always food on the table. My brothers and I wanted money the easy way; we did not want to have to work hard. This is the true story of how our lives turned that faithful day when I walked into the store and stole a whole box of juicy fruit gum.

I was only 12 years old, and I will never forget the feeling I got; it felt good. That was where I first got a taste for crime. Some years later, I remember selling moonshine every afternoon when I got home from school, and I knew there had to be an easier way to make money. One afternoon, as I was walking home from school, I watched this Coca-Cola truck pull into a gas station and pull up in front of a Coca-Cola machine. As I watched the driver, I saw that he had a ring of keys and picked out one of them. Using it, he opened the door and saw what he needed for the machine. As he walked back to the truck, I went over and looked at the key on the side of it; it had written on it the number 52. I just did that out of curiosity, but as it turned out, it was the best thing I ever did.

As I started walking home, the man passed me and pulled into a store where the Coke machines were on the outside. He did the same thing here again, but then he went inside. I again looked at the key. It was the same key that he used across the street. Back then, all you had to do was go to any service station and look on the wall, and most of the time, the keys were hanging on the wall above the cash register because a lot of businesses had their own vending machines. You could use the keys to take what was in the cash boxes in the vending machines. As soon as I figured this out, I started collecting keys.

Chapter 1: Keys and Vending Machines

When I got about 8 keys and found that I could make money by doing this, of course, I told my brothers. We started collecting keys together, and that first weekend, in total, we made about three hundred dollars. This was what we did for about two months - collected vending machine keys. Our first trip out of town was to Montgomery, Alabama, where we worked the bypass, and over that weekend, we made, as I remember, a total of about twenty-five hundred dollars. With my share of that money, I got my first car, a 63 Chevrolet green convertible, which I still love so much.

I started learning the keys. One of the ones I had was a VP Pepsi that was an amazing key; it fit a number of machines; it worked on not only drinks machines but also sandwich machines. I also had an NV that stood for national binding. Later, we went to a vending company and stole a ring of keys from a vending service. Those fit just about everything, and from then on, we worked five days a week just on machines.

Back then, we knew this hustle was going to end at some point, so we started looking at other ways to make money, like from safes at service stations. They had what they called floor safes, and as time went by, we realized just about every business had a floor safe. Some of them were hard to find as they would hide them; they would put rugs or flowers and such on top of them so that no one could see where the safe was located.

When the owner of the store or service station opened the safe in the morning when the store opened, he would be careful not to lock it because he or the manager would be going in it several times a day. So, he would put it on safety instead of locking it. For instance, if the last number to unlock the safe was eighty, he would turn the dial till it reached maybe 99. They would never cross over because that would lock the safe. So, all you had to do was to turn it back to eighty, and then you could turn the handle to open the safe.

A lot of times, it would only have maybe, at the most, two hundred dollars, depending on what day it was and what kind of store it was. We would keep coming back, and if it reached maybe one thousand dollars, then we would take it.

Chapter 2: Safes and Stores

If we were in a town somewhere, for our expenses, while we were waiting to see if a safe ever got any more money in it, we would stay on the outskirts of town checking other stores. To keep our expenses down, we would work vending machines, and that would pay for our motel room. It would always be best to stay in one of the best motels because there are a lot fewer police there. The police would usually be around the cheap hotels where there was usually more trouble.

I remember I was in Saint Petersburg, Florida; at that time, there was a grants department store there. I walked in, and the first thing I did was check and see where everything was and how the office was set up. At that particular one, the office was downstairs, and this was great because it was right across the bathroom. It had a door through which you could see right into the office, and the first thing I saw was a big double-door safe. When you left the first floor and headed downstairs (I guess it was about thirty steps), the safe was right there. I knew I would have enough time to check the safe to see if it was locked or on safety without being seen by someone else. In the middle of the door, there was an opening, so I reached my hand through it and turned the handle, and it opened. Then, before I did anything, I checked the bathroom to make sure no one was in there.

I looked at the top of the steps and then headed into the office and reached the safe. I turned the dial and saw it was on safety. I left it like that and ran to the door to check the steps. It is best to be safe. I shot back in and opened the safe. It had a lot of paperwork in there, and in that split second, I saw a big brown folder. I glanced at it, and I saw money; I closed the door and locked it. I knew if anyone came down, it would take them a few minutes to open it. And anyway, the manager might not have even been there. In any big department store, they came around to each cash register and collected the money they made that morning; all the money went into different places in the folder, so I knew there would be a lot of money in the folder.

After I locked the safe, I knew I had a little time, so I went into the bathroom, opened the folder, and took out all the money; most of it was tens, twentys, a few fifties, and a few hundreds. I took the money and put it in my pockets, wiped the folder off, and put it in the waste can. I then walked up the steps and out the door to my car, which was parked far away.

Chapter 3: Diamonds and Jewels

I left there and drove to another town about fifty miles away and checked into a hotel. Always remember, never check into a hotel where you are planning on working. If I used this tactic, I could spend the night and plan my next move. Most of the time, when you leave your home (mine was in Atlanta), you would have everything already planned out. I was really tired so I went ahead and counted the money because that was the first grant city I ever got.

The place I had robbed was a big department store. There was a total of forty-seven hundred dollars that I had stolen, so since I had just started out on this trip, I went to the nearest post office and sent the money in a package to my home address. I wanted to be safe; I did not want to get stopped with that much money. I insured it for one hundred dollars; that way, I hoped it would not get lost.

As time passed, I started working hotels. Since there were four of us brothers, we all shared everything we found out while working on the road. One of the best things that we learned was while working at a hotel in Jacksonville, Florida.: I stole the passkey, but when you do that, you have to stay away from the hotel for about a month because the police would try to set traps in it to catch thieves.

My brothers did the same thing as me, and about three months passed while we worked hotels. We came to find out the pass key to the Holiday Inn, which I got in Jacksonville, Florida, fit forty percent of the Holiday Inns in the South. From then on, when we got a key, we tried it on other hotels. We obtained a passkey from Jackson, Tennessee, and marked it as J.T. The key from Jacksonville was marked J.F. Finally, we got the passkey to the Holiday Inn in Atlanta, Georgia, which we marked A.G. It turned out that the three Holiday Inn keys fit ninety percent of all Holiday Inns in the South.

The Howard Johnson hotels were good to work; what made them so good was they had a back door. When I work by myself, I would work the Howard Johnson. Back then, all the old people from up North came to Florida for the winter and brought, of course, all their jewelry, like estate jewelry. In the 1930s, many large diamonds were known as "mine cut" diamonds. This term refers to the cut of the diamond, which often features a round opening at the bottom. If the diamond is very clear, it is considered a VVS (Very, Very Slightly Included) stone, meaning it has few flaws visible under magnification. If the diamond has a good color as well, it can still fetch a high price. A diamond that is round is called a brilliant cut. Those are pretty expensive. The bigger the diamond, the more value it has.

If the diamond has any flaws, it goes from VVS status to SI 1 and so on, depending on how many flaws are in it. I remember the first 2-carat diamond ring I got. It was what they call a princess-cut diamond. Now, that is something that makes your heart beat fast; it is so pretty.

Chapter 4: Close Calls

I had breakfast there at the Howard Johnson restaurant, and then I went down Highway 27 until I got to Lakeland. They had a Howard Johnson Hotel and a Holiday Inn, along with a couple of small hotels. Of course, everybody with any money—most of them—would stay at the best hotels. The Holiday Inn was a two-story hotel. I always remember that if you are in a tourist area, always try to watch them check in because they might be with other people.

One weekend, I did not see the tourists check in. When about five o'clock came around, I watched these old people leave their room and head to the restaurant. Well, I did not wait for them to sit down and order their food, which was a big mistake on my part. I took my passkey and went into the room, locking the door behind me. In this case, I was so grateful it was a Howard Johnson. I found an overnight case that seemed to belong to one of the old ladies on the top of the bed, covered by the spread. I knew I was in for some money because if there was nothing in it, they would not try to hide it. I tried opening it, but it was locked.

That was when I heard a key in the door. Someone was trying to get in, so I took the case, went out the patio door, and circled around. I put the case under my arm and walked out. I could see the old people walking to the office to get someone to help them get into their room. I got into my car and drove off. I did not like doing this because if you got stopped, all of the evidence was there to incriminate you.

As I drove, I saw a cheap hotel; I pulled in and got a room. I opened the case, and to my surprise, at the top, there was an envelope. I looked inside it and found two thousand dollars. The case was also filled with jewelry boxes; as I looked, I found that every one of the boxes, from the rings to the charm bracelet, was 14-karat gold.

There was quite a bit of jewelry. I never carried any scales; that would only give the police more reason to search me, so once again, I boxed everything up. I would always carry boxes because a lot of times you had to do things in a hurry. As soon as I was done mailing the stuff home, I destroyed the receipt. I did this because if, by chance, I did get stopped, they could not tie me into anything.

That morning, after breakfast, I drove toward Coco Beach. Sometimes, when I left town, I headed in one direction, but then I got an idea and headed someplace else to execute the idea. If I headed to some city by the Interstate, I always had a backup plan. If you go and work the motels and you don't make any money, then once again you are stuck, and you must go home without any money.

No matter what, I always had a ring of keys. That ring of keys would pay for my hotel room and all my food till I made a score big enough to go home with.

Chapter 5: Tricks of the Trade

I was so tired, so I decided to spend the night in Orlando, Florida. I stayed at a hotel where I had the keys to the vending machines. I really lucked out because a little league team was staying there. All of the kids being there meant that a lot of money was in their machines. I knew I had to be on the ball because they would all be moving at the same time.

That night, at about nine-thirty, I started to work; I began on the fifth floor. Each floor had a Coke machine, and at the bottom, there was a candy machine. I had to finish before the night ended because I would never have a chance to do anything during the day. That night, I got the first one done, then the second floor. I carried a backpack, and by the time I reached the fourth floor, I had to go empty my pack because it was completely full. The machines not only had change, but they also accepted dollar bills. By the time I finished, no one had seen me at all, so I went to my room and went to bed.

It was Sunday morning, so I slept late. I got up, took a shower went downstairs and had breakfast, and checked out of the hotel. No one had seen me, so I knew there was no hurry to leave. So I put the money in different bags. I kept them in the car and labeled them B and B vending.

I left and headed further South. I got to where I wanted to go; I wanted to work at the Holiday Inn. By that time, it was only about 1:30 in the afternoon, so I looked for the nearest shopping mall. I had a few hours to waste some time.

I did not like to arrive too early because all the maids and housekeeping personnel typically got off around five. If they saw you, they would always be there to identify you, while at the same time, the hotel guests would be somewhere up North. If you got caught, they would be far enough away that they would not be able to come and testify against you. However, never count on that. Never take anything for granted because there are a thousand hotels where you can work. What I am trying to say is to never take a chance and always keep your eyes open.

One time, I was at the Howard Johnson Hotel, and my room was facing the front parking lot. A big Lincoln pulled up with an old man and woman; they were loaded down with jewelry, and they had a little dog. As I watched them, it seemed like they wanted everybody to see them; they made a big deal about being there, so I concentrated on them because something was not right. As I watched them, they made one mistake. When the old man opened the trunk, he only used two fingers to pick up the suitcase. Then I knew it was a setup; I never took a chance. Now, a lot of times when they set a hotel up, they already have a man in the room, so when a couple checks into that room and later the couple leaves the room, you see them leave, and you take your passkey and go in. Then, my friend, it is all over; they got you.

When I went on the road, I would always take about four keys because if you have the right keys, they will take care of all your expenses. You have got to keep your expenses down. If you do not, after you get back home and you cash all your gold in, you find you did not make that much. I never went to bars, but sometimes you will make that exception. One time, I was on the road for about two weeks. You get to where you need some company, so that day, I took all the jewelry that I had made in the past two weeks, packed it in a small box that I always carried, and put it in the mail.

I took most of my money and a few other things and went to the front desk and put it in the safe. Then I took the key to where I was staying and got rid of it. You never want anyone to know where you are staying, and I never keep anything in my room except a change of clothes.

I never carried a room key with me. And as I said, I never worked at a hotel where I was staying. But anyway, I tried not to carry anything that showed where I was staying or anything that would lead to my house in Atlanta.

That next morning, I checked out of the hotel, went over to Miami Beach, and pulled into a really nice hotel. When you are on the road, you always work the really nice hotels because that is where the money is at.

It was about nine-thirty, so I found a parking spot. I had on a back pair of slacks, a light blue shirt, and a black sports coat. When you are working high-class hotels, you really have to dress the part. I saw they were still serving breakfast, so I went over and helped myself to some bacon and coffee. At all times, you must always keep your eyes on everything around you. In a place like that, no one asks if you have a room there if you always dress well. So I finished my coffee, headed for the elevator to the top floor, and as soon as I got off, I saw that a family was leaving the room they were checking out of. As I went by them, they started to close the door. The man had his hands full with luggage, so he did not notice me. I put my hand on the door, keeping it from closing. As they got on the elevator, I went into their room; I saw what I was looking for: their room key.

Then I hurried downstairs and watched them leave; they went straight out to the parking area, where a parking attendant brought their car to them.

I went back upstairs to their room. I knew these hotels had room safes; I wanted to see what kind of safes they had. I found it located right behind the door as you came in.

It was the kind I was hoping for; I knew then that all the rooms had the same one - a sentry safe. But at the same time, the fact that it was a sentry safe changed everything.

Chapter 6: The Coin Show

In order to work that motel, I had to have one more person, to be on the safe side. Because I had to have a person watch them go eat or leave the motel.

Whoever I got, we would both be on the phone with earplugs.

For something like this, I got my brother Rob. So I put everything off till everyone got situated, and since this was considered a big score, we worked only the penthouse because this was considered a big hit whether you got anything or not; only the very rich and high rollers would be on that floor. Whether you got something or not, high security would be there the next time, so you had to make this one the best one because we would not get another chance.

Meantime, I went North to exit 44 on the turnpike, got off, and right there at the exit was a Holiday Inn, and right down from there was a Days Inn, so I checked in there. I went and got some lunch and looked around; I passed the civic center; on the billboard, it said World Coin Show.

Now, that was a very good sign. So I went and called the rest of the family, which only three other boys; they knew when I left Atlanta, I was headed toward South Florida. We tried to let everyone know where we would be working; that way, we would not be in each other's way.

But for something like a coin show, we tried to let everyone know; that way, if they wanted to work it, we would take sections. Sometimes, coin dealers stay ten miles away because they know a lot of people would try to rob them; sometimes, it is very dangerous. They have to always be on the lookout for being followed, especially after the end of the show.

So the best time to get them is on the way to the show; that is the only time they feel comfortable because then no one knows who they are. The show would be on a Friday, and that day was Tuesday. So I checked out of the Day's Inn, went about five miles up the road, and checked into a cheap hotel. Now, if the show started on a Friday, most of your coin dealers would get there the day before the show started, so that is the only time we would work a coin show because when the show started, it would be too hard to get them because they would leave everything in what they called lock-up which is a room they put their valuables in with an armed guard.

Back then, most of your hotels were outside hotels, where they could pull up or back up to their rooms to unload their stuff, and in this case, suitcases full of coins. We had tinted windows, and most of the Holiday Inn and Day's Inn were L-shaped. We picked a hotel. Two of us would take the Holiday Inn, and the other two would take the Day's Inn.

Now, since we all had tinted windows, all we did was sit in the back seat and wait and watch. Now, about thirty minutes later, there came a car; I do not remember what kind it was. They backed up in front of their room, got out, looked around, opened the door, and then opened their trunk. This car had a chain to the top inside the trunk, which ran to the bottom. The man put his hand inside, opened the lock, and pulled out a heavy briefcase, then two more, then two suitcases. I called and let them know we had a good chance, so we never took our eyes off that room. Now, there are three things they could do. If they did not eat already, they could order food to their room, load their stuff back up, or, a lot of times, they would come out, look around, and check the cars in the parking lot.

Now they had just got in town, they felt pretty safe, so they would walk to the restaurant up front or walk across the street to Ruby Tuesday. Now that was really good.

I did not have a passkey to that hotel, but I had already checked it, and I took what I call a knocker out of my pocket. Remember, that was a do not disturb that hangs on hotel doors, so as soon as I saw there was no one around or checking in and my brother gave me the word, I took my knocker out of my pocket and put it about six inches above the lock slid it down while shaking the door. I opened it in less than five seconds.

I went inside. At first, I did not see anything, and then I saw the bathroom door was closed, so I went and very carefully opened the door.

The shower curtains were closed; I opened them, and there it was - four big briefcases. I could only take one at a time. I made my way to my car. Always park your car on the other side of the hotel. I put that in the back seat and motioned to my brother, and now we were on a timetable.

We both went into the room, and I got one. My brother was much bigger than I was, so he took the other two; we put them in the car, and as we were driving out, we could see them crossing the road; they had taken to-go orders. You always had to make the assumption that you had to leave right then, but at the same time, just relax just take it easy, and get on the Interstate. Never go over the speed limit; I always go a couple of miles under the speed limit; we were on Interstate 95 to Orlando, and it was getting late, so we decided to check into a hotel. We never drove past nine at night, too many police on the road. They were headed to Atlanta; I wanted to stay and work; I trusted them. After all, we were all family.

Chapter 7: Threats on the Road

That morning, I went to the pool area, sat down, ordered breakfast, and took a dive in the pool; the water was really warm; as I was getting out of the pool, my breakfast came. I needed the coffee,. I always kept an eye on my surroundings; in my business, you have to watch out for everything because some people are doing the same thing you are doing, and the only difference is they do not care how they get their money. My brothers and I do not ever hurt anybody under any conditions, no matter how much money is involved, that will never happen.

Anyway, as I was sitting by the pool, I watched a beautiful young woman walk to the corner of the building and just stood there. Every few seconds, she would glance at me, and I knew right then what was going on: somebody was going through my car.

As I got up, she made a mad dash around the corner. I passed her, and at about that time, I saw a man get out of my car. As I went over there, he did not run, so I knew I had to be awfully careful. I asked him what he was doing. I forgot what he said. I tried to keep an eye on the girl. I motioned for the girl to come over. As she walked over, for the first time, I saw how beautiful she was; she asked if she could do anything for me. Like a dumbass, I told her no, I did not want to get caught in this; I told them if they were working places like this, they needed to head North, I forgot what I told them, but it worked. I watched them get in their car and head North on 441.

I needed a rest, so I headed to the other side of town. I needed to get away from there, so I headed to Tampa. I really like that town; if you go across the bridge, you are in Clearwater, which is a good place to work in the summertime. A lot of people come to Tampa to go to Busch Gardens. I always go there to work.

That time of the year, nothing was going on; only businessmen were in town, so I went across the bridge from Clearwater to the town of Venice, Florida. I was going to go deep sea fishing, so when I checked in to a hotel, I tried to stay away from the front of the hotel, which is always a good habit. That particular hotel was back up to the docks where all the big, real high-dollar boats were. As I walked up the hallway, I noticed a room was half open, and out came two men, acting nervous. They watched me, so I went out the side door and doubled back to see what they were up to. I watched them get in a car with Florida plates. I was so curious I decided to see what they had in their room. I always keep a knocker on me, so I watched them drive off. I went and knocked on the door. I knew I had to hurry. They acted so nervous they might come back at any time, so I looked up and down the hallway. I was so fast with that knocker that it only took a second, and I was in.

I looked under the mattress, but nothing was there, there was nothing there except a pair of pants; as I started over there, I stopped and checked the pillows, and there it was, a package about eight inches long and six inches wide, I knew right away it was a key of coke, I did not mess with it, I was a long way from home, and that carried too much time. So I left it, and I went and looked under them dirty pants, and yes, there it was; I made sure it was money, and then I was on the road again, feeling good. I headed to Interstate 4, going to Orlando, and there I took Interstate 75; I was headed home at about nine that night. I was in Valdosta, Georgia, and knew I had to get off the road at nine. So I got off, checked into a hotel, and laid there and got up and opened the bag I just got and started counting the money. There was a total of 12,500 dollars. That was enough to buy a key of Coke. So what I figured was one of them came to buy that key, and the other had the money, so I sat there just looking at all that money; I felt real good. I was getting really tired, so I put a door stopper under the door, then I watched the news and went to sleep. I got up at about six that morning, took a fast shower, put my clothes in the car, pulled in front of the office, went in, had some coffee, and hit the road. I wanted to go with the flow of the traffic.

Chapter 8: Work Never Ends

After I got to Atlanta, I went home, made some coffee, and put my money in the safe. I had a floor safe; it was right in front of the front door, about six inches back, and I put the carpet back over it. I figured if someone like the police came in, they would step over it, and no one would ever notice it.

The next morning, I got up, went over to my brother's house to pick up my money, went home, put the money in the safe, and called a girl I had been seeing. I told her to pack her clothes; I picked her up, and we drove to the mountains. The next few days were like being in heaven; it was not long before I wanted to get back on the road. After we got back to Atlanta, I dropped her off at her house and gave her a few hundred dollars. Times were rough, and I knew she needed it.

I went over to my brother's house, and he told me my other two brothers were in Alabama working a few motels and machines. They were also working convenience stores, and what they love is grocery stores, which was the best, so I left and went to South Carolina. It was October, time for the snowbirds to head South to Florida. My brothers had to stop somewhere, and after checking all the hotels on Interstate 95, I knew a lot of places they would stay.

I left Atlanta, arrived in Augusta, cut across into South Carolina went through the Savannah River plant; an hour later, I was on Interstate 95, and ten miles up the road was a town called Walter Borough; it was a nice L-shape Holiday Inn. By the time I got there, it was about four-thirty. So on the back and side were woods there I had to be awfully careful; the police would hide in there and watch, waiting to bust someone. So, before I did anything, I walked up the road, cut into the woods, walked about ten feet ahead where I could see the Holiday Inn, and only then did I start walking. I figured if any police were there, all they could do if they wanted was charge me with trespassing; that is a lot better than burglary.

After about thirty minutes, I went and pulled my car where I could see one side where most of the cars were; I climbed into the back seat and waited until about six. An old man and woman left; the restaurant was across from the office. I watched them go in. I waited a few minutes, took my car, and parked it on the other side. I walked back around, walked up to their room, took my key, looked around, and at the same time, opened the door and stepped in. I stood there and looked around, closed the door, and locked it; I could not find anything at first. As I passed the bed at the front, the spread was pulled down, and I looked, and there was her overnight case. I went to look in it, but it was locked, which only meant something good was in there.

So I just took it, I opened the door and looked around and went to the other side where my car was parked. Before I went to it, I did not see anyone, so I got in, drove out, and hit the Interstate going South. I knew I had to get rid of it; it might have their names on it. I was about sixty miles from the state line. I was in that room no longer than maybe five minutes; I knew it would take them about thirty to forty-five minutes to eat and walk back to their room. So, I put my car on a cruise at about three miles under the speed limit.

Chapter 9: Jail Time

I crossed back into Georgia the sign said Savannah, fourteen miles. I drove on to the exit right before you got to Savannah. It was only about eight that night; I pulled through the drive-in entrance at Kentucky Fried Chicken to order a meal and went to check into a motel. I got to my room, took in a change of clothes, then opened the overnight case. I opened it, and to my surprise, it was full of jewelry boxes; the first box I opened, I guess, had about a one-carat diamond ring. I looked in the band. It said 14k. All the boxes had jewelry in them, all 14k. It had a real heavy charm bracelet. It was so much that I decided to head back to Atlanta.

After I got to Atlanta, I cashed my stuff in; it was about eight thousand dollars in scrap gold. I felt pretty good about that, always no questions asked. I stayed in Atlanta for a couple of days.

My brother had a couple of kids; he called me and asked me if I wanted to work with someone. I told him no, but he said the guy we sold our gold to could vouch for him; against my better judgment, I said ok, that turned out to be a big mistake. We went to Valdosta, Georgia; I wanted to work there; I walked around the hotel; that piece of shit I was with did not tell me he and some man worked there three days ago;

if he had only told me, I would never go there, because when you do something, the police would always sets the place up for at least thirty days. And I walked right into it. That is why I like working by myself. He was supposed to be watching, and I saw this old man and woman leave their room, and I went in. There was nothing in the room, and right then, I knew I was in trouble, so instead of going out the backway as I came in, I went through the front; as I wondered what had happened, I did not see him or my car.

When you are working a hotel or just about anything, you leave your keys in the floor of your car, under the front seat. So I did the only thing I could do, and that was head across the street to a shopping center. I made it about halfway in the middle of the road and then they were all over me.

The first thing they asked was what were you doing in that hotel. I knew not to lie; they had cameras everywhere. I told them just a little bit of the truth: I was in the hotel to see someone.

Well, anyway, they arrested me, took me to the county jail, and put me in a holding cell. While I was sitting there, to my surprise, that man that was with me was in the next room talking to a detective. He was still in his street clothes, then he got up, the detective walked him to the side door and let him go.

My time at the Lowndes jail was bad: no air conditioner, no heat; of course, the food was ridiculous; thank God I had money on the books, and I had someone send me some science fiction books. They put me in a tank with about fifty blacks, so you know I had to be careful, but to my surprise, I had no trouble at all.

I played cards, read, and did anything to pass the time, there were some pretty cool blacks in there. I did not like nor want any visitors, so the only thing I could do was just relax, read and wait.

Well, they would not give me a bond; their excuse was I was still under investigation, so at the end of ninety days, they gave me a five-thousand-dollar bond.

I made bond and headed back to Atlanta.

Chapter 10: Never Trust Anyone

I really had not thought much about it, but I had to get home; it seemed like when a person went to jail, everybody wanted to break into their house, so I had to hurry home. I tried not to worry about it much while I was locked up, but now I was really wanting to get home. I knew I had my safe in the best place. I guess now I would see how good my hiding place was.

No one knew where I lived, but there was always someone who knew. I could take a guess, but what good would it do? I would never do anything about it, so I pulled into my driveway. As soon as I did, my neighbor came up with his wife and said, "I missed you." I knew he was just being nosy, so I told him I was in New York, and I decided to stay a few months to help take care of my friend's mother, who was really sick. I did not know if he believed me or not. I did not care anyway.

I opened the door, closed it behind me, went and looked in every room, I had another safe, which I used as a decoy. If someone did break in, they would most likely take it. I would leave a couple of hundred dollars in it, and they would never think I had another one. So, no one, as far as I could tell, has been in my house. I made some coffee and tried to figure out the best way to go about finding out more about that man I was on the road with.

I went over to Carl's house, a good friend of mine; after I talked with him, he said he had known him for about two years; he never suspected he was undercover working with the Atlanta police department, so I never doubted him. Carl and I had known each other since we were kids, so the only thing I could do was let it go. Then I started going out; my favorite spot to go was the Holiday Inn lounge, where I started going out with the bartender. Her name was Julie, we started going everywhere together, just enjoying each other, then I made a big mistake, I asked her to marry me, we planned on being married, and then out of the blue, she started asking for expensive things.

I was really in love; I got her a new car and new clothes, and then she started acting funny. I told her I had to go out of town, so about three days later, I called her and told her I would be gone about four or five more days; she said okay, that was a lie. I was already back; I wanted to see what she did when I was out of town. As soon as she left, I had someone follow her. I had to get in the house, open my safe, and take everything out.

I never told her anything about the safe or where it was, but I wanted to be safe. I took everything over to my brother's house, went down to his basement, put everything up behind a false partition, and locked it.

Then I got a call from my friend who was following her; she was at a cheap hotel, and I told him to get pictures of the door and make sure his camera had a date and time stamp. That way, it would hold up in a court of law.

Chapter 11: The Betrayal

I knew something was going on; she knew I had money, and I think she had a boyfriend, and I think they were going to rob me. Then, if they did that, I knew they would kill me.

So I picked up my brothers and some friends from their houses; I did not want them to see any cars but mine in the driveway. I knew it might be today since I was back in town after about a week, and she knew I would have money, so my friend set up cameras all over the house. As I said, I do not believe in violence; that is why I had five people with me to make him not do anything.

And besides, all of this might be for nothing.

Just then, two cars pulled into the driveway. Four men got out of the second car, and a fifth man got out of her car. I did not expect this; I was looking out the window and saw a gun in one of their hands.

I told my friend to go ahead and call the police and tell them we were being robbed. She tried to come in, but I had the deadbolt on with a chain; she asked me why I did not open the door. I told her to hold on; I was getting dressed, and there was someone here who needed to talk to me. I looked out the window, and the biggest black man I had ever seen was looking me right in the eye, so I closed the curtains. I told her just a minute, and then one of them said hurry up, man, I have to use the bathroom. At about that time, the police showed up. Then I waited, and three more cars of police showed up. That was the first time I ever wanted to see the police.

They asked what was going on, I told them, and they asked if anyone was carrying a gun; the girl spoke up and said it was her house too; that is when I lost it. I told the police she moved in about two months ago and I go out of town a lot, and when I do, she goes over to this man's house. Then she started calling me a no-good liar, so I went and showed the police the video. I could have waited, but I wanted to get this woman out of my house. And then he asked the man with the gun, what are you going to do with this? The black man said it was for his own protection. The best thing was was not have a gun permit.

So, the police put the man with the gun in the back of the police car. And the girl left with that big-ass black man. After they left, my older brother went and rented a UHaul truck; I was leaving as soon as I could. One of the police pulled back into the yard; I told him there was no way I was going to spend another night there. He said that was the smart thing to do.

He also asked if that girl knew where any of my friends lived. I told him no.

Chapter 12: My New Home

After he left, we finished loading the truck, and I went over to the floor safe, there was nothing in it, so I filled it up with liquid cement. When we left, we made sure we were not followed, and then we called it a night. Atlanta is a big city; you could be on the F.B.I. ten most wanted list, move to the other side of town, and be lost to the world.

That next day, I put my house up for sale; I gave it to a real estate company and gave my home address in New York City. I gave them power of attorney, so as far as anyone would ever know, I never existed.

Anyway, I went to the other side of Atlanta. I had someone rent me a house, and everyone helped me unload the Uhaul.

As I wondered about that girl, I could not understand how I fell into that trap, but I am glad it turned out the way it did.

I had a friend go over to that car lot where I got her car. They still had the title, so my friend talked to them, and they put a pickup order on that car. I told them not to take any money just pick the car up.

While all of that was taking place, I went over to my new house, and my friend and I put in a new floor safe. Then he put in all the cameras and set them up so he could monitor everything from his house.

I promised them I would never bring anyone to my house or let them know anything about my friends. About a week went by, and they found my car and went and picked it up. I never saw her again, and to me, that was a blessing.

That is the end of that story, and thank God for that.

I was wondering where to go, and then I thought about Miami, so I told my brothers all about it. I did not like to leave out any details because this was a big deal; there was no telling how much money and jewelry would come out of that hotel with all the rich people from all over the country living there. I was the very best one when it came to opening doors; I was that good and fast, with a knocker. But they had something else going, so I told them I could wait, I would work someplace else, just let me know when they were ready.

They said they had something going on in Mississippi and wanted me to come, but I liked working by myself, so I asked them to leave a message at a place we all used; that was before cell phones came on the market.

I left Atlanta on Interstate 20, which would take me right into Florence, South Carolina. They had a Holiday Inn there, and they were building a Hampton Inn right down from a Cracker Barrel. It was only one o'clock in the afternoon, so I decided to go South about thirty miles. There was another Holiday Inn there that was set up well, meaning on both sides, it was all swamp, no one could hide there. Before I left Florence, I had some lunch and took my time. They also had a rest area, so I pulled over and killed some time; I did not want to get there before five o'clock because the maids would still be working.

Chapter 13: Terrible Restaurants

I pulled in, and all the maids were gone; that only meant one thing: they were not busy. The day was Wednesday, and I had to work there. I did not have time to go anyplace else. As I sat there, a Lincoln with an old man and a woman pulled up in front of a room, and the old man got out and guided her in.

I was in the back seat of my car where no one could see me because I had tinted windows, so I watched them unload. They went inside, and about thirty minutes later, they came out, got in their car, and drove off. I knew the only restaurant was about ten minutes from there, and it was a very good place to eat. So I gave them about five minutes and headed to that restaurant, and sure enough, they were there, so I went back to the hotel and parked my car on the other side, then took my pass key, which we called the Atlanta key, and went in and I locked the door behind me.

I looked around, and I went to her suitcase first; on the side was a zip-up compartment with two envelopes. They both had one thousand dollars inside and on the side of the bed was an overnight case. It was locked, and it was a samsonite case, and I had a key that would fit it. A Samsonite key would fit almost all of them. I opened it up, and all you could see were jewelry pouches. I opened one up, and it was full of gold rings; there was no need to waste time, so I just took the case and left to walk around to my car, made sure no one was around and left.

Interstate 26 was about five miles from where I was. I looked at my watch, and by that time, they were gone about 15 minutes, so I figured it would take them about thirty minutes to eat; if they got it to go, it would be about twenty minutes. I would never stay in a room for over five minutes, and if you cannot find anything by then, you better leave; you never know about people. I got on Interstate 26. It took about two hours to get to Spartanburg and check in to the nearest hotel; I still had to go through all that jewelry; as soon as I got off the Interstate, I pulled through a drive-up window and got some fish and went and checked into the Hampton hotel.

I like this hotel. The free breakfast is worth the extra money; you can eat there plus take a sack lunch.

Also in the overnight case was another bank envelope with five hundred dollars. By this time, I was feeling really good.

Most of her jewelry was rings and gold bracelets; I never carried any type of jewelry on me or in my car.

I carried in my trunk a few post office boxes, and as soon as I left, I went to the nearest post office and put it in the mail; as soon as I got outside, I tore the receipt up and then headed home.

I was about fifty miles from Atlanta, and I was getting hungry, so I got off the exit and saw a Davis Brothers cafeteria. I pulled in, found a parking space, and went inside. I went through the line, got my dinner and coffee, found a table, and sat down to eat. In my words, what is this? It was ice cold, and the mashed potatoes and gravy were so bad. I took my food up to the cashier and told her I wanted my money back; she said with a super nice voice that she was very sorry, but she could not do that; the manager was gone for the rest of the day.

I did not want to make a scene; I never wanted anyone to remember me, so I said thank you very much, and I left. I got to Atlanta, went home, and checked with my friend. He was the one who kept watch on my house; I paid him three hundred dollars a month, whether I went anywhere or not. He was severely handicapped, but most of all, he was my friend.

Chapter 14: Bingo

That next morning, I picked my friend and his wife up. As always, when I got back in town, we had breakfast together, and then we dropped his wife off and went to see our friend; he is my friend's brother. He likes to come along. Sometimes, he will buy something, and at Christmas, he gives it to his wife. We sell everything as scrap gold. And everyone is happy.

So after we finished, I dropped my friend off at his house and went to pick up some things, like groceries; I was going to be in town for a couple of weeks. I enjoy movies, just watching TV and relaxing. You may believe it or not, but this is a tough job; you have always got to be on the lookout for anyone who looks at you twice; they may be the police or someone who thinks you may have something, but they are too lazy to work and too nervous to steal. I try to take a lot of pride in everything I do. A lot of times, people I know ask me to open something, and we have an arrangement; I charge so much up front and sometimes 10 percent of everything in the safe. Sometimes I have to wait for my money, but that's okay, I do not mind. I was fooling around the square in downtown Marietta and went into a magic shop, and right away, I thought about that Davis brothers cafeteria; they would not give me my money back, so

I looked around and found the perfect thing. I guess I hated to do it, but they should not serve food that was no good. I went back to my house, fixed me some chicken and dumplings, and settled down and watched TV.

For the next few days, I spent time with my mother; she was a beautiful Christian woman; she never knew what we did, she loved us boys so much, she would always pray, and she really enjoyed going to Church. I loved her so much.

After spending time with my mother, I went over to my brother's house and talked to them about their schedule and Miami Beach.

The motel was five stories high; the first floor was meeting rooms where they played bingo, the second floor, we would not work because it would be easy for someone to come up the stairs to the room. If bingo lasted forty-five minutes, I figured we would only have about twenty minutes to work.

That would put one person on the elevator and one person in the doorway, leaving two people to do each room, which would cut the time down. Once we finished that floor, the man who watched the elevator had the most important job. When we finished the top floor and moved to the next floor, if he saw the elevator go to the top floor, that was when we had to leave immediately. Chances were they would not miss anything at that moment, but we never took a chance.

So the day came. We went in three cars. We spent the night in Fort Lauderdale at the Day's Inn. It was Friday morning, and since we did not have a passkey, I brought about ten knockers since I was the one responsible for opening the doors. I gave myself thirty seconds to open each door; if I could not, then I would move on to the next one. Bingo started at seven, and at seven fifteen, we were on the job.

In the first room, we went in, there was a jewelry box sitting on the dresser, so the only thing I did was look and make sure everything was real. My brother, who was with me, had a backpack, and as soon as I said it was real, he would take it and pour it into the backpack; about twenty minutes later, we finished that floor. And then we were running out of time, so we decided not to press our luck, so we left.

The backpack was full; we got on the turnpike and headed toward Orlando, where we would spend the night before it got too late. So, at about ten, we pulled off the road and got a room at the Day's Inn. I glanced at all the jewelry, and I think we had more jewelry than most stores.

As we opened the ring boxes, the first thing I saw was what appeared to be a two-carat diamond ring.

We had no way to gauge the size because we never carried anything with us. We never gave anyone a reason to search our car. If they opened our trunk and saw anything, they would really look; and if they thought drugs were there and saw scales, that would give them probable cause to search our car and, of course, take everything they wanted.

Chapter 15: My Mother

The next morning, we packed everything up, put everything in three different boxes, put enough stamps on them, and put Happy Birthday on them; that way, it would take a search warrant to open the boxes. We all went and had breakfast and started that long trip to Atlanta.

My brothers and I have talked about this so many times before. We know people who have so much money that the only way to get it is with a gun, but we know if you start down that road, the only thing that is waiting for you is prison, and you will never see the outside again, and it is not worth it, not for all the money in the world. If you have to take someone's life, it is not worth it.

We got on Interstate 75, which would take us all the way to Atlanta; late that afternoon, we pulled into my driveway, and I told them just go ahead and separate all the stuff, and I would see them tomorrow afternoon; they would go through everything and separate the diamonds.

That night, I went to Kroger to get some groceries. I had no plans to go out of town. I called my mother to ask her if she would like to go out for dinner. She loves catfish, and I love red snapper, and I knew a great seafood restaurant, so I told her I would pick her up at around seven. I have two other sisters, so I invited them; I do believe everyone enjoyed their dinner. It was a Louisiana style restaurant, so I ordered on the side a bowl of shrimp gumbo; I had never had it there, but it turns to be very good, so I ordered my mother one, and she really loved it. That made me feel really good to see the smile on her face. After I dropped my mother off and started home, I just could not help thinking about what a wonderful mother she was. I remember growing up, we never worried about anything, we had a great family, there was always plenty of food, we never went hungry, and my stepfather worked really hard. But as for me doing what I did, I liked it. And the more I did it, I just wanted to be the best. I took a lot of pride, and if I wanted to learn something like opening locks, then I would take a course in it.

On the road, while I was working, I would never carry my locksmith license with me because that would be a charge by itself, and then I would have all kinds of detainers on me from everywhere.

The only thing I carried with me was one pick and one tension bar, which is a must, and finding the right tension bar for me was the main thing; you have got to have a really good one. Also, I took with me about 10 knockers; I have already told you about them, they can really make you a lot of money. You never know when you will need one.

I headed to Kentucky. I always like to stop at that Corvette museum right when you cross the state line; I always like to go when they run the Kentucky Derby; so much money. I remember one time I pulled into a restaurant just off the Interstate; as I was parking my car, a big Lincoln pulled up, and a young man and woman got out of their car, went and opened the trunk, and put their purse in it under a blanket. I watched them and waited till I could see where they would be seated; in the meantime, I went and parked my car on the other side of the restaurant, and then I went to see where they were seated. It was perfect. I went back around, and I did not see anyone, so I jumped on the back bumper a couple of times; I did that because if it was a factory alarm, the alarm would not go off. If the alarm went off, then they added a proper alarm to it. Anyway, with a factory alarm, you could break all the windows, and the alarm would not go off; now, if you added an alarm system to it, as soon as you break the glass or jump up on the bumper, the alarm would go off.

Chapter 16: Deserving or Not?

I always carried a bag with me, this one I got from the Cracker Barrel. I went and looked everywhere I did not see anyone. I took a small bottle of WD40 and sprayed it in the lock, then took my pick and raked it four or five times, and then took my pick and started from the back to the front and, at the same time, put a very little pressure on the tension bar easing it to the left. That opened it. I looked around one more time, and then I opened it; the alarm was going off. I pulled back the blanket, and underneath it was a money bag. In a situation like this, you take everything. Now, on most alarms, the horn would go off in about thirty to sixty seconds.

So, by the time I got in my car, the alarm stopped going off; it must have had a 30-second alarm. Nobody paid any attention to it. I tried not to make any unnecessary changes, so I got off at the next rest area and opened her purse first; wow, I just got myself the biggest diamond solitaire I had ever got. Also in her purse was five thousand dollars in cash. That was all except pictures of horses, so I guess they might have had one in the race.

Now the money bag had a padlock on it, so I just took my knife and cut the top off, and oh my goodness, after I counted it and with the other money, that was a twenty-five thousand dollar hit, not counting the diamond. So back to Atlanta I went.

When I crossed the Georgia state line, it was about nine-thirty; it was time for me to get off the road. The next morning, I just got myself some coffee and got back on the road. After I got back in Atlanta, I took that diamond out of the setting and took it to my friend; the diamond turned out to be what they called an SI 1; in other words, it was not the best, but it was damn good.

My real father was dead. He died of cancer, and my stepfather was good; I had nothing to complain about after I took care of my business. I remember I was at the Holiday Inn on Howell Mill Road in the lounge, where I go just about all the time. I was going with the bartender; she was very beautiful and really smart. I met her one night over in Buckhead while playing poker. She was hostess and also worked for the man who ran the games; at that time, he ran everything. I will never forget her; nothing was ever talked about on the phone; she told me her boss wanted to see me. I guess I have known him for about five years; he knew what I did. I did a couple of things for him over the years. I met him that night, he wanted me to do something I have always been against. At first, I told him no, then he told me Judy owed him a lot of money, that she borrowed it for her family and never could pay him back. He told me he would drop everything she owed him plus pay my five thousand dollars.

I told him no, I would never do anything like that. He said OK, and I left; from that day on, I never saw her or talked to him again. I do not run drugs or sell them. Now, everyone knew that, and if they ever came around me, they would never talk about drugs. And I like that.

I did hear a few months later on the news, young women. It never said her name, but it said she was caught speeding and high on drugs. They searched her car and found fifty keys of speed, and I guess the reason I did not hear from him, or if it was my friend, was because of the DEA. They made a deal with her. You only have to get caught one time, and then it is over; everything you got, they take.

One time about four years ago, I was lonely, I guess; I went on Facebook and got to talking to this one girl. I just wanted someone to talk to, but the more I talked to her, the more I got to like her; she lives in Los Angeles, California, and she told me she was thirty-two years old; the more I talked to her, the more I really like her. She was from Toronto, Canada; the more I talked to her, I did not know what it was, but I found out that when she was two years old, her mother and father were killed in a car accident. She has only one sister, and at that time, her older sister was in California; the younger sister, the one that I like, was still in Canada; that is when her sister came and got her. Since Kate was a child, all everyone did was take advantage of her. She had a second-grade education, and I could imagine what that poor girl went through.

Since her sister came and got her, it has been four years now. I have been sending her two hundred dollars a month; her sister now keeps her in the house and never lets her go out. And I am getting ready to go get her. I have got to make just a little more money because I want to send her to school and get her a little house in the mountains where no one could ever run her off. I guess that is going to take a little more money; now I guess I have got to go back to work.

Chapter 17: Ethics in Thievery

Most of all my money went to gambling girls, and I guess I had so much that I did not care; it was like living in a different world. All the people you meet live in the same world you do. But of course, they did different things but went to the same places you go. The money came so easily, and all of a sudden, like overnight, you wake up, and everything has changed.

You pack up a few things and get ready to leave town, and you have breakfast with your family like you always do. This time, I would head to Savannah, Georgia. I guess it was about three o'clock. By the time I got there, I got coffee, and by that time, the maids had got off work. So I drove around and checked the hotels out, and wow, I just got the biggest surprise I had ever got in my life; they were changing the locks on all the hotels in that area; that did not bother me… by that time in my life I could just about open anything.

Now, here comes the surprise: they were putting new locks on the doors. They called them card keys. They work the same as the other keys, except every time you check in at the hotel, they would make you a key right when you check in. And when you check out or as soon as your stay is up, it will be deactivated.

Take it with you or lose it; it would be no good no more. The perfect lock.

I could still get them with a knocker, but there is nothing like having a key. So I went about fifty miles North, I was going to work in South Carolina, but I did not make any money, so I decided to go back home and relax and do something different, and start all over again.

After I got back to Atlanta, everybody was out of town, so I decided to relax and work around the house for the next week while they were gone; they built a new outlet mall, so I guess I just wanted to check it out and pick up some things. I guess it was late afternoon when I got there; just as I pulled in, I just happened to see some man come out of a furniture store carrying a briefcase. At first I thought it might be a salesman, but not on a Sunday. I watched him put it in his truck and went back into the store. The car was parked in a good location, so I wanted to see what he had.

The car did not have a factory alarm, or the lights would blink, so I looked around. So, as I went by the back of the car while no one was around, I jumped on the back bumper, and the alarm went off; they added an extra alarm to it; if they had a factory alarm, the alarm would not go off if you broke a window, only when you open the door, an add on alarm would go off if you did anything to the car, so much for that, so I went shopping instead.

I picked up some pots and pans and some kitchen utensils and headed back home. I went by T.G.I. Fridays, and got some food for dinner, and I guessed since no one was at home, I would watch football and just relax.

That next morning, everybody started to arrive back in town. Everyone comes back at about the same time, and when everyone leaves town, everybody knows, so we do that because if something goes wrong and we do not hear anything, we know where to start looking because sometimes they do not get a chance to call if they get in a jam.

When someone is working out of town, everyone knows where they are working. So if we have to start looking, the first thing we do is clean up his house; that means everything. Because the first thing the police do is run to their house and look for anything they can use that can put them in jail for a long time or that can help them in other cases.

Lucky for us, he was okay; he just got stranded changing a tire coming across the mountains in North Carolina, where there was no phone service.

It was the 4 of July coming up this weekend, so I decided I would work the machines in Montgomery,

Alabama, on the bypass; they had about fifty machines, and everyone was an A.R.A. Machine, and I had the main keys, the last fourth of July we pulled out about two thousand dollars. Money was so easy to get; you never think about tomorrow; you always think about how much I know and all the knowledge that I worked so hard to learn. And I thought I knew just about everything, and you will see I did not know anything..

Well, anyway, my brothers and I left Atlanta 2 hours later; we were in Montgomery, there was all four of us brothers were going to work together; it would take us about three hours, 2 of us started on the other side of the bypass, we would all meet in the middle. One person was looking, and the other person worked the machine; the first one I opened was a sandwich machine.

One thing I like about this vending company is that they collect every Monday morning; this was a holiday weekend, it was eight o'clock Sunday night, it should have had a lot of money in each machine, the first one I opened, since it was a holiday weekend, they refill the machines, and did not take any money, the money that was already there, they put in brown bags, and they must have sold out because all the bags were half full some of them were already full.

Just by looking, the first machine had about two hundred, and we started to work feeling really good. We had to get every machine because everything would be gone, or the police would be patrolling the area, so we had to make this run the best because we could not come back here for a long time.

Two brothers started on one end, and my other brother and I went to work on the other end. About four hours later, we met in the middle. It was a total of sixty-five machines, so before it got too late, we headed back to Atlanta.

That next morning, we counted everything, and it was a total of eighty-five hundred dollars. Twenty one hundred dollars, and the other hundred we took out for gas, not bad for four hours of work.

One thing I am proud to say is that we never took anything from anyone who could not afford it, and once again, we never believed in any kind of violence.

It was the first of the year the fun show was held in Orlando, Florida. It is one of the biggest coin shows in the South. We had enough time to get ready for it. I really like it; I love to go in and look at all the coins that people find in the mountains, on the beach, it is so much fun if you really want to take your family to the eight wonders of the world, you should take them to Cordele, Georgia in about June or July and see the millions of watermelons you drive through the gates and the first thing you see is about one hundred men waiting to try to get you to hire them to load your trucks, then you will see school buses with the top cut loaded down with watermelons, that is why I call it the eight wonder of the world.

It was 1995. I thought while I was waiting, I would run over to Interstate 95 and see what was going on. The first place I went was the Howard Johnsons, which was a great place to work; it was only about eight-thirty in the morning. I had plenty of time, so I went and checked into a hotel across the street and went to bed.

I got up at about 4 in the afternoon, took a shower, and went to get some lunch because it might be a little bit before I could eat.

So, by that time, it was about 5, and all the maids were going home. So I drove over and pulled in, and there were about six cars already checked in. I did not care anything about them because I did not see them check-in. You have to watch everything because two people might leave, and somebody might still be in the room. I like to watch them check in; that way, you know how many are in that car and what they look like.

There were about ten cars. They all looked good, and I waited, and when one left, I would go in and lock the door behind me; that's why I love this hotel. They have a back door.

I went over it real good; they did not have anything, so I waited for the next one, and there they went, still nothing; I guess all in all, I went into about six rooms with nothing. At about eight that night, I watched a family of five check in. I guess they wanted to stay in the best hotel; they had saved up their money all year, so they all left. I just wanted to see what they had and went in. I felt so sorry for this family; I found his wallet. It had three five dollar bills, so I reached in my pocket, pulled 2 one hundred dollar bills, and put them in there with his other money; then I left and went back to my hotel and watched some TV. I was a total of three hundred and ten dollars in the hole, but I felt good about it. At least I made a family have a better vacation.

Chapter 18: The Little Church

Well, I finally went to court on that other charge. Well, it was my fault, so I could have put it off, but I wanted to go ahead and get it over with.

The judge gave me four years, and I would get a letter from the Department of Corrections telling me where to report.

Well, about a month later, I received a letter from the Department of Corrections telling me where to report. I had to go through Jackson first; that is where they have death row. Jackson was a diagnostic and classification state prison.

I spent eight weeks there; I was lucky I was on kitchen detail; I had to be careful; I could eat just about anything, and the officers ate completely different food. But the bad side of working in the kitchen is if you get caught, then you will go to the hole and not work in the kitchen anymore. So, to be on the safe side, I stayed away from their food; it was not worth it.

I liked Jackson, but that was what they called supermax; they did not play any games, and the goon squad would come in and beat the hell out of you most of the time for no reason. Well, it finally came at four in the morning. They loaded me up, along with

20 other prisoners. And I was on my way to Wheeler, a private prison; they make a lot of money, they are on the New York Stock Exchange, but anyway, after we went through orientation, they assigned me to dormitory orderly, which was an easy job.

As days go by, you look back on your life, and you wonder what happened. Your life is gone, and you have nothing to show for it. Now you are in prison with no hope for the future, just the same old thing, nothing new. That is what makes a person so lonely no matter how strong you are, and I do mean mentally, but a person has got to believe in God, and just doing that, he will be able to overcome all the dangers that lay waiting for him.

I like to say I have believed in God all my life, but like a lot of things, I took it for granted. They say when a person goes to jail, they turn to God just as a way to get over everyone until they are released on the street, and then it is the same thing all over again. I do believe in the good Lord; it kept me going all the while I was in jail. I slept in a cell with 15 other prisoners, and I always had to keep one eye open.

Then, after 2 years, my time finally came; that morning, they called me to receive and discharge. I dressed in civilian clothes, and gave me 25 dollars and a bus ticket, which I did not need. I had someone pick me up. I remember stopping at Denny's restaurant, and of course, everything was so good.

As days went by, I did not want to do anything, I do not know what it was; I guess I just did not have it in me anymore. And then by that time, all my brothers had passed away, and I had COPD, and I decided I did not want to ever go back to prison; I did not want to die in there; now I am getting old, I have cancer, and after all the money that I had made, over the years I was going to die broke and homeless.

With nothing to do, I walked down to Cumberland Mall and went into Books Are Us. I picked up a coin world magazine to see what was going on; the nearest coin show was about 2 months off. I had a little expense money left that I always keep for emergencies, and I needed something now, so I found a car show in Waycross, Georgia that weekend. It was a three-day show, so I left on Thursday and got there at about three in the afternoon.

There were three hotels there, two inside and one outside. I wanted to work the outside one; that way, I could sit in my car in the backseat with tinted windows, and I was good to go. At about eight that night about six cars came in with stickers on them, with pictures of cars on them. I saw a man and a woman get out of their car. He was carrying a briefcase, and I knew he might be the one I needed to get. About an hour later, they came out and went straight to their car and put the briefcase in the trunk; that was good. It was a Lincoln; with my pick, of which I only carried one, I could open it easily. Now, if it was factory when the alarm went off, it would be on a 30-second cycle. They walked across the street, and I gave them about ten minutes. Nobody was out, so when I opened it, the alarm would go off, giving me enough time to reach in, get the case, and move back under the balcony. Then it would go off, and if anyone looked out, all they would see was a car with the alarm going off, and they would pay no mind to it; they go off all the time.

After I got it, I walked around the hotel, got into my car, and hit the road. It was a two-lane highway all the way to Valdosta, so I pulled into a truck stop, opened the briefcase, and there were two money bags. I opened one, got the receipt out, and did the same to the other one.

I had gloves on, so I pulled out, and just before I hit the road, I threw the case in the woods across from the truck stop. I headed to the Interstate; I guessed I had about thirty minutes, and that would put me in the safe zone. The money was from the gate and the concession stand.

After I got on the Interstate it would take me four hours to get to Atlanta, then I would see how much money I made. I was thinking about how quick it was to open that Lincoln; sometimes it is that easy, and sometimes it is so hard. That is why I always carry a small bottle of WD40, you put it in before you do anything. A little straw and WD40 will work miracles. Take your pick and run it back and forth two or three times, and that makes all the difference; then it will open so easily.

After I got to Atlanta, I went straight home and, made some coffee and put all the money on the table; there were two thousand in one, and the rest was a total of 65 hundred dollars, which was not bad. I was so tired of being alone. I needed a partner, one I knew was gone or dead, so for the next few days, I had to figure out where I should go and work for the next few months.

I got on Facebook and started talking to a girl; she lives in Los Angeles, California, and we hit it off really well. I was thinking about sending her a plane ticket and maybe buying a house somewhere in the mountains; she is thirty-five with no education, so the first thing when I get a house, I will put her in school. I got to have the house paid off; in case something happened to me, she would always have a place of her own.

She is like my daughter; I am 79 years old, and everything in the world is wrong with me.

Now, I need a big score; I think about two hundred thousand would do. I never save anything, but now I have to come up with something good.

I remember a few years back, someone was telling me that a white van would come around and pick the money up, starting from Macon, Georgia. He also told me about the owner. The man had three trucks working seven days a week.

I did not jump into anything; I had to know more. I was thinking about trying to find the house where he used to live and start from there.

I found the house, and a little boy about ten years old came out and asked me who I was looking for. I told him the name of the man I used to know. He told me that was his father. So, I was right on the money. A few minutes later, a man came out, and he recognized me and, threw up his hands and was glad to see me.

When I first met him, I told him my name was John Leavins, so I left it that way. Better to be safe than sorry. I asked about the job where they pick up the money three times a week, the last one was on a Sunday, and he told me everything was the same.

I always tried to check everything out, but I needed the money so badly, and I thought I could trust him because my brothers had worked with him a few times. It was Sunday morning. I was waiting at his last stop when he went into the store and came out with nothing, so I was really confused; I turned and looked at that guy beside me and asked when was the last time he checked everything out, and he looked at me like I was stupid, the only thing he said was he didn't know what happen, but the only thing I knew was I spent all my money for nothing..

I asked him when was the last time he checked this place out; he told me two years, and I almost lost it. But it was not his fault. It was his mind. So I dropped him off at home and started back to my house. But I had the list of the places where they were supposed to pick up the money. So, with nothing to do, I went to one of the places that he had marked off, and with nothing to do, I just waited.

About an hour later, I watched the truck pull up, and he got out and went inside; about ten minutes later, he came out with a big bag; he opened the back door and put the bag inside; it looked like it was really heavy, and he pulled out and hit the Interstate. He did not stop until he reached a row of warehouses right on the edge of town. He pulled up, got out, and went to a box on the side of the door; he opened it up, cut the alarm off, and went inside, and then the big roll-up door started to open, and then he came out and pulled the van in.

I parked my car around the corner and walked by the door he left open. I did not see him, but I heard a lot of noise in the back, so I just walked on in. I saw him in the back inside an office where he was at a big double-door safe, and he was busy doing something, so I backed up, took a few pictures, and left the way I came in. I stayed in the car a few minutes and watched another van pull in, which we did not know anything about, and then the first man we were watching drove out, got on the Interstate, and left; it was about five-thirty in the afternoon, I waited for about an hour no one else showed up.

So I went and picked that guy who put me on this; I told him we needed a third person, I told him everything I had seen, and that we should get it tonight. I wanted that third person to go and sit somewhere where he could see anybody coming and warn us on a walkie-talkie.

I got the tools that I was going to open the safe with. The back of the building was all wooded, so all these buildings were put together with sheet metal screws. No windows. That was a good thing.

There was an apartment complex not far from there, so we parked the car and went into the woods. I guess it took us about ten minutes, and there it was. The trees were right against the building, so I took out my quarter-inch nut driver, and about twenty minutes later, we had the first layer off, and now we were in.

Motion detectors were everywhere except in the office. So I was about ten feet off, so I put the side back on that I took off and started again. This time, I hit the office dead center. We went in kept low, and on the floor were bags of quarters, which was weird, so I went to the safe, and this was hard to believe it was on safety, I guess because all the vans that came and unloaded, so I opened it up.

There were about fifty money bags, and about twenty bags of quarters, about two thousand dollars in all. I remember on the way in; I saw a grocery cart; I told him to carry as many bags of money as I figured we could take all the bills at one time, get the cart, and come back for the change.

We took all the bags and put them in the car, then went back for the rest of it. It was really hard trying to get that cart through the woods; we decided to come back for it because it was getting late, and we needed to get off the road. But in the morning, these woods would be crawling with police, so we took what we could and tried to hide the rest of it.

By the time we got home and counted it, we had forty-one thousand in bills and 17 hundred in quarters. After we split up, I was lying in bed as always. I was really lonely; a lot of times, I wanted just to end it, I guess, because I found it hard to be around people.

I got up, took a shower, and kept thinking about my life; it was like I had nothing to live for. I got dressed, and heading out of town, I went North on the Interstate with no particular place to go. I crossed into Tennessee, and by that time, I was feeling so bad I started to cry for no reason at all. I pulled off at the next exit and pulled into a roadside park; I was feeling so alone and depressed I just wanted to end it. I used to read the Bible a lot, but nothing ever came of it. As I sat here, I wondered about God and thought about what I was fixing to do, and I guess I was afraid to go on in this life; nothing seemed to matter; the more I thought about it, I could not do it, I could not hurt myself, I knew the good Lord would not forgive me. So I headed back on Highway 41 to Atlanta still with a heavy heart.

I was going to go over the mountain; I could save about thirty miles going this way. I guess it was about four in the afternoon. I was going through a small town somewhere in Tennessee, still trying to find that shortcut back into Georgia, when I saw a sign that said dinner in the valley. Well, I was really hungry, so I pulled in; there was nothing that could beat good country cooking. I noticed a preacher standing at the door of the Church, motioning people to come in and pray and give thanks to the good Lord. As I watched, a young girl came up and smiled, took my hand, and said welcome to your Church.

The people in that country Church were so nice. It was like a family I had never had. I really enjoyed being there and meeting all these wonderful people. As I talked to several people, I felt right at home, and I decided right then this was my new home and this was my family. I really did not have anything in Atlanta to go back for except my clothes and my money, so before I left, I went around talking with everyone I knew. This is where I wanted to spend the rest of my life; I already fell in love with this place, and all the people here were my family.

So, after dinner, I said goodbye to everyone and headed to Atlanta; what I was going to do first was count my money. I figured I needed to be on the safe side with at lEast 130,000 dollars. So I drove all night, and I got there at about eight that morning. I went straight to bed. In my safe, I had sixty thousand dollars and about two thousand in quarters.

I would never hurt anyone, no matter how much money somebody had; if you just took your time, you could make a world of money, and you would never have to pull a gun or hurt anyone.

There is really only one place to go for loads of money, and that is Miami; you got your drug money, not counting all the thieves in the world; they all come to Miami. All you have to do is be in the right place and keep your eyes open, and it will come; you just have to be ready.

I only brought with me one thousand dollars. I hoped that would be enough; it would take about one fifty a day just in expenses. I was in no rush to get there, so if I saw anything, I would try to get it, but I never took any chances. I got off at exit 44 on the turnpike. I was going to get on Interstate 95 into Miami.

It was about time for the maids to get off, so I liked to watch people check in; that way, you knew what to look for. I never liked working with the young crowd. You never know when they might run back to their room, and you get a big problem, so I stayed with the older crowd. I was sitting in the back seat of my car. No one could see me because of the dark tint I had on my rear windows.

I sat there for about an hour when an old Lincoln pulled in. I do not pay much attention to the cars that pull in; I watch the people, see how they dress, and I go from there. So, after they checked in, I watched them go to their room; I made sure I knew what they looked like, then I went and waited and got where I could watch the exits, and then I sat in my car and waited. That way, no one could see me walking the hallways because there was no need for that. And I did not want anyone to see me.

So, about twenty minutes later, they left; they walked next door, and as soon as they went in and sat down, I took my knocker out of my pocket and made sure no one was in the hallway, and then I went in. I found their jewelry and money, and they only had about six hundred in cash and about three hundred in gold, so I left it. I did not like to make the place hot for a few hundred dollars.

I worked till about eight that night then I decided to call it quits for the night. So I did well because no one had seen me, and I could work there the next day, so I left and went to find myself a Day's Inn motel and spent the night. As I pulled in, I just happened to see a man and I woman come out of a room. They looked very suspicious; the way they looked around and acted very nervous; they went to their car and unlocked the trunk. As I watched them, they put a blue bag underneath some clothes and walked off.

As soon as they went in, I had my WD40 in my hand, put a little in the keyhole, and raked it a couple of times, and as soon as I put my pick in, it opened. I looked around and opened the trunk, looking under the clothes where there was the blue bag. I opened it up and saw a jewelry box. Inside was a diamond solitaire of about two carets and an envelope with some money in it; I was going to keep it anyway, so I closed the trunk and walked around to the other side of the hotel where my car was parked. I left and headed on to Miami.

From where I was, it was only 70 miles to go; then I would be in Miami. By the time I got there, it was about ten that night, so I checked into a hotel and looked over the stuff that I just got. That diamond was from what I could tell, was a really nice stone. I would know more once I got back to Atlanta.

Now I opened the envelope, and what a surprise, there were thirty 100 dollar bills. So, first thing in the morning, I found a Wells Fargo bank and deposited it in the ATM. That way, I would not have that money on me. I tore up the receipt, went to the post office, and mailed that diamond to a person I knew in Atlanta.

Now I was going to South Miami to a place where everybody goes. I wanted to find a good inside hotel where I could keep watch on everyone that checked in. Also, if the police were watching everybody or had it staked out, then they would have to get inside with you, then you would still have to keep your eyes open for anything.

The rooms here were 140 Dollars a night, so before I checked in, I needed to go inside after the maids got off. I brought three keys with me. They fit just about all your Corbin locks. I had about an hour left before I could check my keys, and I also wanted to look at the inside of the door.

This was a nice Holiday Inn. It was a five-story hotel. I went in the side door. I took the elevator to the top floor, and no one was around, so I knocked on the door at the end of the hallway. I waited a few minutes and tried my keys, and the first one fit; it was what we called the Jackson because that is where we got it: Jackson, Tennessee; as I said, there are only three main keys, and I had them all.

As I waited downstairs at about six that evening, a beautiful four-door Lincoln pulled in, and four elderly people were checking in, so I waited till the bellhop carried their luggage to the top floor. They had two adjoining rooms, so I went down, got in my car, and waited.

At seven, they all came out, got in their car, and drove off. So I took the steps to the floor they were on. Nobody was in the hallway, so instead of knocking, I took my key and went in; the adjoining room door was open, so I glanced around the room and I saw a briefcase on the side of the bed. It was locked, but it was a new one, so that meant if they did not change the combination, then it would be on 000. It was.

I opened it up, and the first thing I saw was a fat money bag. I opened it up, and all I could see was banded 100-dollar bills.

I found her bag, and there were five hundred dollars lying on top. I looked around and found his black satchel, and inside was a black bag with all one-hundred-dollar bills; I knew this was the best day I had in a long time.

I gathered up all the jewelry and took the elevator to the second floor and then took the stairs to the parking lot.

I got on Interstate 75 till I got to Fort Lauderdale and got on the turnpike doing the speed limit. I got to Orlando; I decided to go ahead and check into a hotel before it got too late.

I checked into a Holiday Inn and got a room on the bottom floor. I counted the money out of the first room. There were thirty thousand dollars, the second room, forty thousand dollars, that was seventy thousand dollars total, oh yes, the five hundred dollars, then the jewelry, I would figure that out when I get to Atlanta.

After I got to Atlanta, I went through all the jewelry, and I sold everything, including the diamond, which turned out to be a 2-carat, which was what they called a VVS stone.

Including everything, I had one hundred and sixty thousand dollars. So that was all I needed, so I loaded up everything I had and headed to that little town in Tennessee. I got there that night, checked into a hotel, and the next morning, I went and paid one hundred and ten thousand dollars; it was bought from an individual, a really nice three-bedroom house setting on a mountain top. It was a fantastic buy.

That afternoon, I went down to that little Church, and as I pulled up, that same girl came out along with the preacher, and right then, I knew I had a family and a home. I give all my thanks to the mighty God in Heaven for giving me a new life. Amen.